FIRST AMERICANS
The Iroquois

SARAH De CAPUA

Marshall Cavendish
Benchmark
New York

ACKNOWLEDGMENTS

Series consultant: Raymond Bial

Benchmark Books
Marshall Cavendish
99 White Plains Road
Tarrytown, New York 10591
www.marshallcavendish.us

Library of Congress Cataloging-in-Publication Data
De Capua, Sarah.
The Iroquois / by Sarah De Capua.
p. cm.—(First Americans)
Summary: "General overview for young readers of the Iroquois people.
Covers history, daily life, and beliefs. Contains recipe."
Includes bibliographical references and index.
ISBN 0-7614-1896-2
1. Iroquois Indians—History—Juvenile literature. 2. Iroquois Indians—Social life and customs—Juvenile literature. I. Title. II. Series:
First Americans (Benchmark Books)
E99.I7D29 2005
974.7004'9755—dc22
2004027575

On the cover: Young girls wearing traditional costumes at a celebration in Montreal, Canada.

Title page: A traditional Iroquois longhouse in upstate New York.

The artwork on page 28, by Arnold Jacobs, represents The Great Tree of Peace growing from Turtle's back, Eagle, The Great Guardian of Peace, and Elder Brother the Sun.

Photo Research by Joan Meisel

Photo credits: Cover photo: Martha Cooper/Peter Arnold, Inc.
Arnold Jacobs/Two Turtle Studio: 28. *Corbis*: Nathan Benn, 1; Bettmann, 12, 35; Bowers Museum of Cultural Art, 19; Royalty-Free, 20; Werner Forman, 30. *Getty Images*: MPI, 8. *Marilyn "Angel" Wynn/Nativestock.com*: 6, 14, 23, 24, 33, 39. *North Wind Picture Archives*: 4, 10, 11, 16. *The Philbrook Museum of Art, Tulsa, Oklahoma*: Richard W. Hill, Tuscarora (b. 1950), *Clan Mother*, 1977, watercolor on paper, museum purchase 1977.1.2, 18. Tom Two Arrows Dorsey, Onondaga (1920-1994), *Creation Legend*, c. 1946, watercolor on board, museum purchase 1946.24, 26. *Photo Researchers, Inc.*: Lawrence Migdale, 38; Ray Ellis, 40. *Peter Arnold*: Martha Cooper, 31, 36.

Map by Christopher Santoro
Book design by Symon Chow

Printed in China
1 3 5 6 4 2

CONTENTS

1 · WHO ARE THE IROQUOIS PEOPLE?

The Iroquois live near the Great Lakes in Wisconsin, Pennsylvania, and New York. Some live in Oklahoma. Many also live in Canada, in the provinces of Ontario and Quebec. They number about seventy thousand.

Six different tribes make up the Iroquois—the Cayuga, Mohawk, Oneida, Onondaga, Seneca, and Tuscarora. Long ago, these tribes were enemies. But by the end of the 1600s, the Cayuga, Mohawk, Oneida, Onondaga, and Seneca had united and formed one nation. Around 1712 the Tuscarora joined the nation, called Haudenosaunee (Hoe-de-no-SHOW-nee). This means People of the Longhouse. A longhouse was a building where many families lived together. The people are also called the Iroquois League, or the Six Nations. Their

An Iroquois settlement on Manhattan Island during the 1500s.

enemy, the Algonquian, may have given them the name *Iroqu*, which means rattlesnakes. The French who came to North America called them "Iroquois."

The Iroquois lived along the lakes and in the forests of the present-day northern United States and southern Canada. The center of the Iroquois League was near present-day Syracuse, New York, where the Onondaga lived.

The flag of the Iroquois League.

This map shows the traditional homelands of each of the five original members of the Iroquois League and where the Iroquois live today.

Hiawatha (in canoe) brought peace to the warring Iroquois tribes.

Deganawida and Hiawatha

The Iroquois League was started when a Huron leader had a vision that the tribes could live in peace. His name was Deganawida. The Iroquois call him the Peacemaker.

Deganawida met with Hiawatha, an Onondaga leader. Hiawatha agreed with Deganawida. Together, they traveled from tribe to tribe, bringing their message of peace to the original five nations of the league. They convinced the tribes that they would be stronger if they stopped being enemies. Deganawida and Hiawatha gave the people thirteen laws they should follow. If they all followed the laws, they would have peace.

The tribes agreed with Deganawida and Hiawatha. All the tribes came together and formed a new government. As the Iroquois League, the tribes began protecting each other from enemies and spreading the laws of peace to other tribes.

Leaders of all six nations would meet to make important decisions and rules that everyone in the league followed. The Iroquois League was very powerful.

In the mid-1600s fur traders arrived in North America from Europe. They traded metal weapons and tools with the Iroquois, who gave them beaver furs. Soon beaver fur

European traders arrived in the mid-1600s. Here, they trade with the Iroquois along the Hudson River.

was very popular in Europe. Europeans began trading with other Native American tribes for the fur. Some of these tribes were the Iroquois's enemies. Fighting broke out between the Iroquois and these other Indian tribes. Many Iroquois were killed in the fighting. Diseases such as smallpox brought by the Europeans killed thousands more.

Many Iroquois lived in the forests of Canada.

By 1740 nearly half the Iroquois population had died.

Throughout the 1700s more and more colonists arrived from Europe to live permanently in North America. French colonists helped western tribes fight the Iroquois. The Iroquois made friends with British colonists. The French and British were enemies. So the Iroquois helped the British fight

The Iroquois joined the British in their fight against the French in the French and Indian War.

the French. That war, called the French and Indian War, lasted from 1754 to 1763. The Iroquois and the British won.

By the 1770s the American colonists wanted to form their own country and be free of British rule. The war between the Americans and the British was the American Revolution. It was fought from 1775 to 1783. During this war the Iroquois tribes disagreed for the first time in many years. Most Iroquois fought with the British. Some sided with the Americans.

When the Americans won the war, the Iroquois League was shattered. The newly established United States government wanted Iroquois land for its own people. Most of the land the Iroquois lived on was given or sold to the United States government. Sometimes the Iroquois were tricked into signing treaties that gave their land to Americans. A small part of their land was set aside as a **reservation**. A reservation is land that the government gives Native American tribes to live on. In Canada these lands are called reserves.

These Iroquois League chiefs, photographed in 1910 in Ontario, Canada, were from the deer and turtle clans.

During the 1800s the U.S. government forced many Iroquois to move to reservations in the Midwest. In the early 1900s the government tried to discourage the Iroquois from speaking their tribal languages and following their traditions. Many Iroquois children were sent away from the reservations to attend boarding schools.

After the 1920s, reservation life began to improve. The U.S. government spent more money on reservation hospitals and schools. Children were able to stay with their families and attend school on the reservation. In 1924 the Iroquois, and all Native Americans, became U.S. citizens. Native North Americans in Canada became Canadian citizens in 1951 where they are called First Nations Peoples. Other Americans became interested in native cultures. The Iroquois were proud to share the customs and traditions that make them the People of the Longhouse. They continue to practice and share their culture today.

2 · LIFE IN THE WOODLANDS

Iroquois villages were made up of several hundred to as many as a few thousand people. Villages often were built near streams or rivers, where fresh drinking water could be found. The Iroquois were farmers. They grew corn, beans, and squash. These crops were so important to the Iroquois that they were called the Three Sisters. The Iroquois also grew tobacco. Villages varied in size, from just a few longhouses to a few hundred longhouses. Villages were surrounded by a high wooden fence for protection.

Villages were made up of family groups called clans. A clan is a group of families who are related through the mother. The Iroquois have nine clans: Bear, Beaver, Deer, Eel, Hawk, Heron, **Snipe**, Turtle, and Wolf. Each clan was led by a woman, known as the clan mother. The clan mother was

The forests that surrounded Iroquois villages provided cover for hunters, who often hunted deer at night.

in charge of choosing the clan's chiefs. If she thought the chief wasn't doing a good job, she could remove him. She also made sure everything ran smoothly in the longhouse and in the fields. Clan mothers were not the only powerful women. All the women managed the land and crops. They took care of the longhouses, prepared the food, and looked

This illustration shows a clan mother surrounded by animals representing the different clans.

after the children. They also made clothing out of animal hides.

Men were in charge of clearing the land so the women could plant the crops. They hunted deer, moose, and caribou. They also trapped rabbits, squirrels, and porcupines. They fished in the nearby rivers and streams. They caught bass, eel, salmon, and trout. During times of conflict, they protected the villages. Iroquois men also were in charge of repairing the longhouses, making tools and weapons, and trading with

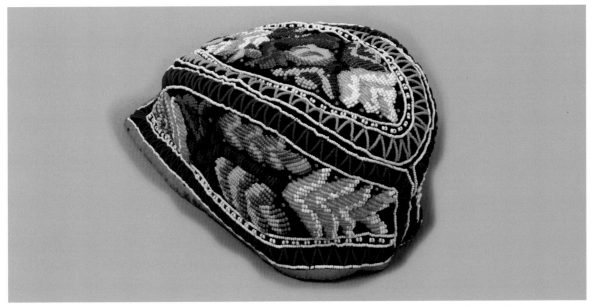

This beaded hat is an example of the clothing Iroquois women and girls made.

Ogwissimanabo (Yellow Squash Soup)

Ask an adult to help you prepare the following recipe. Wash your hands with soap and water before you begin.

Ingredients:

- 1 medium yellow squash, diced
- 4 shallots, chopped
- 1 quart water
- 2 tablespoons maple syrup
- 5 slices cucumber (1/2 inch thick)
- 1 tablespoon salt
- 1/4 teaspoon black pepper

Place the squash, shallots, water, and syrup into a large pot. Simmer over low heat for 40 minutes, or until the squash is tender. Add the cucumbers. Remove from the heat and put the mixture into a large bowl. Mash until it forms a thick, creamy paste. Put the mashed mixture back into the pot. Season with salt and pepper. Simmer for 5 to 10 minutes. Serve hot.

other tribes and, later, the Europeans.

Iroquois girls followed their mothers. They learned to plant crops, make clothing, and prepare food. They helped the women gather wild berries, nuts, and fruits. Around age eight or nine, boys began following their fathers and other male members of the clan. They learned to hunt, fish, make tools and weapons, and trade.

The longhouses of each village were about 50 to 150 feet (15 to 46 meters) long. They were 18 to 25 feet (5 to 8 m) wide. Longhouses had curved roofs and low doorways at each end. All the members of the same clan lived in a longhouse together. An image of the animal that stood for each clan living in the longhouse was carved above the doorway. Longhouses were made of curved wooden poles covered with elm bark. Cracks in the bark were filled with tree sap. There was a row of holes in the center of the roof. These let out the smoke from the fire pits inside. Each family had an area of the longhouse to themselves. Areas were separated by sheets of elm bark. Clay pots, wooden bowls, snowshoes, and dried corn and meat hung from the **rafters**. Platforms for sleeping were built along the inside walls of the longhouse. People slept on cornhusk mats. They used bearskin blankets in the winter.

In addition to farming and cooking, women made the clothing for their clan. Most of the clothing was made from deerskin. Women sewed together pieces of deerskin with

An Iroquois longhouse made of elm bark.

This Mohawk girl is wearing the traditional dress of her people. This photo was taken in 1901.

needles made from animal bones. In warm weather, men and boys wore only a breechcloth. A breechcloth is a piece of deerskin run between their legs and tied at the waist. Women and girls wore knee-length skirts. During the winter, all the people wore deerskin shirts, leggings, and moccasins. They also wore robes made of bear, deer, elk, or moose skin, with the fur on the inside for warmth.

Women decorated the clothing with porcupine quills and dyed moose hair.

Men and women wore necklaces, bracelets, and earrings made of stones, claws, shells, and bones. Women and girls braided their hair. Men and boys usually shaved one side of their head. Some men shaved both sides, leaving a row of hair on top. Today, this style is known as a Mohawk.

After the arrival of the Europeans, the Iroquois began to make their clothing out of cloth. It was easier to sew and faster to make into clothing than animal skin. Iroquois women used ribbons, beads, and sashes to decorate their outfits.

Each village had its own leaders, and each tribe had a council. Clan mothers chose members of this council. The tribal council was in charge of making laws for the tribe. The tribal council also chose members of the Grand Council. Following the Great Law of the Iroquois League, the Grand Council met in late summer or early fall at Onondaga. The council made sure the league's laws were followed.

3 · IROQUOIS BELIEFS

Traditionally, the Iroquois were very religious. As is true of most American Indians, the Iroquois believed that all things on Earth had a spirit. Gods called Creator, Our Grandmother the Moon, and Our Elder Brother the Sun all lived in Skyworld. The earth rested on the back of Turtle. Corn spirits watched over the villages and crops. Dreams were important to the Iroquois. They believed that whatever they dreamed would happen to them.

The Iroquois held many ceremonies, which followed the seasons. The four major seasonal ceremonies were called Midwinter, the Planting, the Green Corn, and the Harvest. During these ceremonies, people offered thanks and danced in celebration for their crops. The Sun and Moon ceremony included shooting arrows at the Sun during the day and at the Moon at night.

This painting, created by an Onondaga artist, illustrates the creation of the world.

How the Earth Was Made

Long ago, in Skyworld, Skywoman was gathering nuts and berries. She fell through a hole in Skyworld. She tumbled through the air down toward where there was no land. There was only water, where fish and animals swam. As Skywoman fell, swans and geese flying over the water caught her with their wings.

"What shall we do with Skywoman?" the birds asked. "She cannot fly like we can, and she cannot swim. She needs a place to stand."

The creatures decided they should dive into the water and bring up soil from the bottom. All tried and failed, except for Muskrat, who brought up a tiny bit of mud.

"But where shall we put it?" the animals asked.

"On my back," Turtle said.

So the animals placed the bit of mud on Turtle's back. It grew larger and larger until it became the earth. There they put Skywoman down. She dropped the nuts and berries she was carrying from Skyworld. They grew into all of the plants and trees of the earth.

Skywoman's children became the Haudenosaunee.

An Iroquois False Face mask.

Tobacco was burned so its smoke would rise into the sky.

In the spring and fall, a group of men would form a group called the False Face Society. Wearing masks to frighten away the evil spirits, they walked through the village. All of the society's members were men, except for one woman. She was known as the Keeper of False Faces.

At different times throughout the year, especially in winter, the Iroquois believed that evil spirits brought disease and illness to the village. A **medicine man** would perform ceremonies to drive the bad spirits away.

Each important event of an Iroquois's life was marked by special **rituals**. In all events, the Iroquois had to show they were brave. Men proved their bravery in battle. Women proved their bravery in childbirth.

The birth of a girl was celebrated because she would grow up to have babies and add more people to the clan. Baby boys were welcomed by the tribe because they would grow up to be strong, brave hunters who protected the village. Babies were named by the clan mother. As the babies grew up, they received

Today Iroquois continue to perform the ceremonial dances of their ancestors.

many different names. A person could have as many as six different names in their lifetime. But no name was held by two living people at the same time.

When girls were about twelve or thirteen years old, they were given their own cooking pots and utensils. They cooked and ate their food alone until they married a young man from another clan. When boys reached the same age, they were sent into the forest alone on a **vision quest**. They ate no food for about two weeks. This was to cause them to have dreams that would tell them what they would become when they grew up.

In some Iroquois tribes, a young man's mother would suggest a wife for her son. If the young man liked her choice, his mother spoke to the young woman's mother. If the two mothers agreed their children should be married, they asked the clan mother. The clan mother's decision was final. If she said no, the marriage did not take place. If she said yes, the young man and woman exchanged gifts to mark their engagement. At the marriage ceremony, the bride brought corn bread. This meant she promised to be a good Iroquois wife. The groom brought meat. This meant he promised to provide food for their family. They lived in the bride's longhouse, with her clan. Iroquois couples usually married for life. They did not think divorce was good for the clan. However, if the husband did not provide for his wife, she could order him to leave the longhouse. Or she placed his clothes, weapons, and blankets outside the door. Both were free to remarry.

Medicine wheel gardens like this one are sacred places where healing plants are grown.

Handsome Lake, whose Seneca name was Kiontwogky

Disease and war meant the Iroquois did not usually live long lives. Nearly half of all children died before the age of twelve. Adults lived until about age thirty. Burial practices varied by tribe and changed over time. Early Iroquois placed the bodies of the deceased on wooden platforms high above the ground. This brought the dead closer to Skyworld, where the Creator, Our Grandmother the Moon, and Our Elder Brother the Sun lived. After the body broke down and only bones were left, the bones were buried. Each village had its own burial ground.

The Iroquois believed that the dead person's spirit wandered the village for ten days. They held the Tenth Day Feast with food, tobacco, and songs. This feast was believed to protect the living and help the dead person's spirit reach the Land of the Dead. Twice each year, the Iroquois held the Feast of the Dead to help any spirits still wandering the village to leave on their trip along the Path of the Dead. This path led to the Land of the Dead.

Around 1800 a Seneca leader named Handsome Lake introduced a new religion. It was called *Gai'wiio* (guy-we-oh), or the Good Message. The Good Message was a mixture of **Quaker** and traditional Iroquois beliefs. Handsome Lake told the Iroquois to stop drinking alcohol, strengthen their families, share among themselves, and farm as a way of life. Many Iroquois still follow the Good Message, which is now called Handsome Lake's Religion. Today, most Iroquois people follow either Handsome Lake's Religion or Christianity.

4 · A CHANGING WORLD

About seventy thousand Iroquois live in the United States and Canada. They are U.S. or Canadian citizens, as well as members of the Iroquois Nation. Some live in cities and towns away from the reservations and reserves. Many Cayuga and Mohawk live on the Six Nations of the Grand River Reserve in Ontario. Mohawk people also live in Kahnawake and Kahnesatake-Oka in Quebec. The Oneida live on small reservations in Wisconsin and New York. A few Seneca live on reservations in Pennsylvania and Oklahoma. The remaining Seneca, Tuscarora, and Onondaga live on reservations in New York state.

The Iroquois do not live in longhouses anymore. Each family lives in their own home. But at least one longhouse stands in each Iroquois community. It is where religious,

Mohawk children prepare to go kayaking on a lake on the Kahnawake Mohawk Reserve in Quebec.

social, and political activities take place.

The seasonal ceremonies of Midwinter, the Planting, the Green Corn, and the Harvest are still performed by some Iroquois. Women still head clans. Councils continue to meet and make decisions for the Six Nations, based on the Great Law of Peace. Traditional dances and crafts are still practiced.

Onondaga gather to perform a ceremonial dance on their reservation in New York.

The language of each of the Six Nations is still spoken, as well as English. Some Iroquois in Quebec also speak French. Clan mothers still name babies.

While many of the traditional ways of life are still followed, the Iroquois live in the modern world too. Iroquois

The game of lacrosse was created by Native Americans. These Onondaga boys take a break during a game.

children go to schools on the reservations, as well as in cities and towns away from the reservations, where their parents work. Many work as teachers, doctors, lawyers, and business-people. Mohawk steelworkers are especially well known. For more than one hundred years they have worked high in the

A Mohawk steelworker helps to construct a building near New York City.

sky, building skyscrapers in the United States and Canada. These so-called skywalkers seem to have no fear of heights, and walk across **girders** easily. Some Iroquois raise cattle or grow fruit for a living. Others are artists, writers, and musicians. Many adults work as guides for tourists, or in casinos.

In recent years, the Iroquois have experienced greater interest in their culture by non-Indians. As People of the Longhouse, they share their traditions with others to preserve their way of life.

· TIME LINE

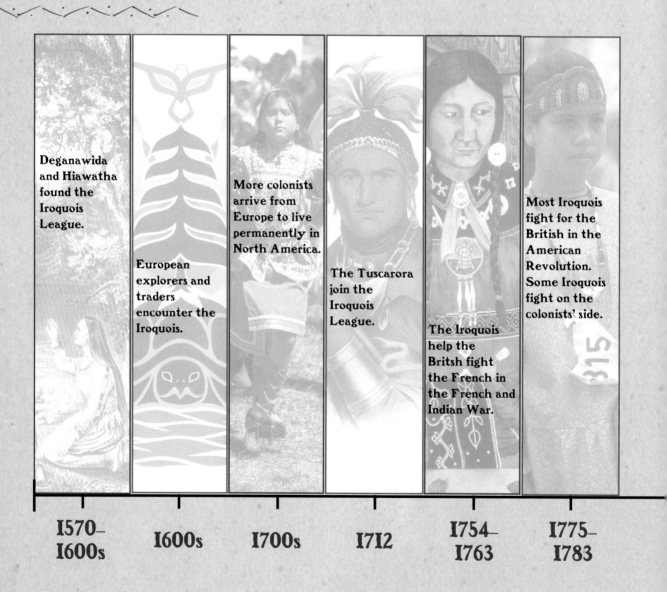

Deganawida and Hiawatha found the Iroquois League.

European explorers and traders encounter the Iroquois.

More colonists arrive from Europe to live permanently in North America.

The Tuscarora join the Iroquois League.

The Iroquois help the Britsh fight the French in the French and Indian War.

Most Iroquois fight for the British in the American Revolution. Some Iroquois fight on the colonists' side.

1570–1600s

1600s

1700s

1712

1754–1763

1775–1783

With American success in the Revolution comes the breakup of the Iroquois League. Iroquois lands are taken over by the Americans.

Seneca leader Handsome Lake founds the Good Message, now called Handsome Lake's Religion.

The U.S. government forces the Iroquois to move to reservations in the Midwest.

The U.S. government tries to discourage the Iroquois from speaking their languages and following their traditions.

U.S. Congress passes a law making all Native Americans U.S. citizens.

Reservation life improves for the Iroquois, who proudly share their tribal culture with non-Indians.

The Canadian Parliament passes a law making all Native people in Canada citizens.

1783

1800

1800s

1870–1920

1924

1930–present

1951

· GLOSSARY

girder: A large, heavy beam made of steel or concrete, used in construction.

medicine man: A Native American healer.

Quaker: A Christian group founded in 1648 that prefers simple religious services and opposes war.

rafters: Beams or supports that hold up a roof.

reservation: Land given to Native Americans by the U.S. government; called reserves in Canada.

rituals: Ceremonial acts or actions.

snipe: A marsh bird with a long bill and brown feathers with black-and-white spots.

vision quest: Rite of passage in which a Native American youth journeys alone into the wilderness to seek spiritual guidance and direction.

Books

Gunderson, Mary. *American Indian Cooking Before 1500*. Mankato, MN: Blue Earth Books, 2001.

Press, Petra. *The Iroquois*. Mankato, MN: Compass Point Books, 2001.

Shenendoah, Joanne and Douglas M. George. *Skywoman: Legends of the Iroquois*. Santa Fe, NM: Clear Light Publishers, 1998.

Takacs, Stephanie. *The Iroquois*. Danbury, CT: Children's Press, 2003.

Web Sites

www.civilization.ca
This is the site for the Canadian Museum of Civilization, located in Gatineau, Quebec. Here you'll find online exhibits about the history of Native people in Canada.

www.iroquoismuseum.org
The official site of the Iroquois Indian Museum. Visit in person or online to see the collection of art and objects that illustrate Iroquois society and culture.

www.nmai.si.edu
For an online tour of the newest addition to the museums of the Smithsonian Institution. The National Museum of the American Indian opened in September 2004. Here you can view the museum's exhibits of Native American art, crafts, and more.

Sarah De Capua is the author of many books, including non-fiction, biographies, geography, and historical titles. She has always been fascinated by the earliest inhabitants of North America. In this series, she has also written The Cherokee. Born and raised in Connecticut, she now calls Colorado home.